main outside. Even for you the door may be suddenly shut; th⸺ your death, perhaps unexpectedly, who knows how soon? Or ⸺ returns, for that too may be soon. If you have not e⸺. Think of what it will be to stand before a closed d⸺

Outside is wailing and gnashing of teeth and t⸺ only entered when I read that booklet about *'House of Gold⸺*

Which sentence describes your situation?

I AM INSIDE *or* I AM OUTSIDE

Which of these statements can you erase? Have you enough courage to answer truthfully? The door is still open. Christ is still waiting with outstretched arms, saying, 'Come unto Me with your sins, *Come!'*

THE ALTAR OF BURNT OFFERING

Someone is approaching; one of the people, an Israelite. He is ill at ease and restless. He has with him a sheep on a leash. What urges him to come? It is his fear of God! He has sinned, and his conscience is troubled. He knows about the Holy God Who lives in this House of Gold.

Should he run away from God, in the opposite direction? No, you cannot flee from God. To even think of this righteous God causes the man to break out in a sweat.

The court

The man keeps coming, along the north side of the white curtain wall. Its purity affects his conscience. He comes to the east side. There he sees the wide open gate. He hesitates no longer, but enters. Now he stands in the spacious court. In front of him rises that beautiful house, the House of God, impressively high. The sun burns on the sand of the court. He feels as if he were standing in the light of God. He feels that God is looking right through his clothing into his heart, that God knows everything about him.

A priest approaches him. 'What is the matter with you?' the priest asks. The man stutters, 'I ... I have sinned ... and ... God ... must punish ...' 'Yes,' the priest answers, 'You have come to the right place.' God had all this prepared specially for sinners, not for people who think they are good.

Altar and offering

'Just follow me.' And then they stand near the first object of the tabernacle: the large, brazen altar of burnt-offering. The word 'altar' means 'place of sacrifice'. We wouldn't even dare to guess how many animals have been killed and burnt at that place. Throughout the entire Bible we are told about the meaning of the altar and the offering. It speaks of Christ and His work of atonement on the cross. This is the focus of all God's thoughts and the only ground of salvation for sinners.

The altar and the thousands of offerings brought throughout the ages give an impressive picture of the perfect Sacrifice of Christ and His work of redemption on the cross. From eternity to eternity, the cross of the Redeemer is the central point between heaven and earth.

God's plan

God knew beforehand what would become of creation. He knew the plans of the devil who wants to ruin everything that is of God and destroy not just creation but the life of every individual in his desire to drag all with him into everlasting destruction. But long before, God had a plan in His heart whereby He would save men. Only *God* could think of such a plan.

He is the Holy God, Who could not condone sin or let it go unpunished. God *is Light*. (1 John 1:5). He had to judge man *righteously* and punish him. But if He did so, how could His *love* be shown? God is *Love* (1 John 4:8,16). Then God unfolded the plan: His own Son would go down to earth and become Man, to die in the place of guilty sinners ...

Throughout the Old Testament, each altar and each animal offered as a sacrifice, pointed to God's beloved Son and to the way in which, one day, He would come to earth to suffer and die on that awful cross.

Dying in the place of ...

'I notice that you brought an animal for sacrifice!' says the priest to the man with the sheep. 'Yes, I knew I must. Must the animal really die?' 'Certainly, for without the shedding of blood there is no forgiveness possible,' (Heb 9:22). 'But this animal is innocent! And my children are so fond of it. This sheep hasn't done any wrong, has it?' 'That is just the point. One guilty person can never take the place of another. You have forfeited your life through your sin. Now *you* must die, or an innocent victim must die in your place.'

'Lay your hand on the head of this lamb; for in doing so, you will admit that you are guilty and the lamb is guiltless. God views this act as your identification with the lamb for sacrifice. Your guilt is transferred to the lamb. When the lamb dies, you will be free and guiltless as the lamb was before.'

Quietly, the man puts his hand on the head of the lamb. There are still a few preparations ... the knife ... and then, the blood of the lamb flows in the sand of the desert. It is a solemn sight. Yet, while the man sighs deeply, lifting his eyes momentarily to heaven, he feels a great burden slipping from his shoulders. The lamb died instead of him. 'And it shall be forgiven him' (Lev 4:31). 'O, God, I thank Thee.'

What about you?

May I ask, have you, reader, young or old, ever drawn near in thought to the cross of Jesus in this manner? He, the Holy One, the sinless One, He suffers beyond description. He dies. This is the suffering of Christ as a substitute. For whom?

Not for *all* men. Thousands are indifferent to the cross. They merely continue to live, either in degradation of sin or in conceit, but nevertheless, irrespective of the fact that Someone died for them, until their own death when they are lost forever.

Others have looked, fascinated and affected, but they have never come to God as that Israelite came, as sinners.

Christ died for all who have laid their hand on the lamb, the Lamb of God. You may, do this too. You may do it with hands together, saying softly to Him that hung on the cross 'I, too, have sinned, I deserved that cross, Lord Jesus, where Thou didst die in my place.' Then you may lift your hands up to heaven and say, 'O God and Father, I thank Thee, I believe Thee, I trust the work of Thy Son accomplished on the cross. And I thank thee, in the name of the Lord Jesus.'

At that moment, God will forgive all your guilt through the blood of Christ. You will be free, eternally free!

> In the cross I glory ever.
> Can the law condemn me? Never!
> Christ became a curse for me.
> Christ has died on Calvary,
> From both sin and death I'm free,
> Christ has purchased life for me!

How large was that altar?

The priest takes the lamb and carries it to the altar. Only then does the man have a good look at the altar. It is 5 cubits long and 5 cubits wide. This is certainly not by sheer chance.

In the Bible, five is the number of responsibility. The law has five commandments covering man's behaviour toward God and five covering his behaviour toward his neighbour (Ex 20). We have five fingers on each hand and five toes on each foot. What have I done with my hands? Only good things? In all my actions and activities I am accountable to God. Where have our feet taken us? Only to places where God wanted us to go? In all the things for which we must account to God, we have failed. We are guilty of breaking every commandment, with each hand and each foot. Nobody has lived up to God's requirements. We have transgressed not a few but all God's commandments, if only in thought!

Anyone who accepts the truth of this may come to God's altar, to the cross. Here hangs the perfect Man, Jesus Christ, the only One Who during His life on earth obeyed all God's commandments. That is why He was the only One Who would do the work of atonement and present the sacrifice to God.

The altar had four sides. There are four seasons, four points of the compass (Isa 11:12). In the Bible, four is the number of the earth. That is why we saw four colours in the Gate and why there are four gospels that speak of the Saviour of the world Who came to earth for all. He is 'a ransom for all', meaning that He is available to all (1 Tim 2:6).

Everyone that wants to be saved can be saved.

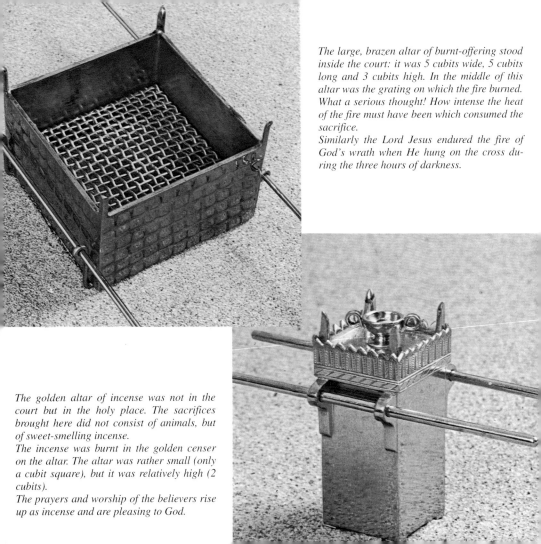

The large, brazen altar of burnt-offering stood inside the court: it was 5 cubits wide, 5 cubits long and 3 cubits high. In the middle of this altar was the grating on which the fire burned. What a serious thought! How intense the heat of the fire must have been which consumed the sacrifice.

Similarly the Lord Jesus endured the fire of God's wrath when He hung on the cross during the three hours of darkness.

The golden altar of incense was not in the court but in the holy place. The sacrifices brought here did not consist of animals, but of sweet-smelling incense.

The incense was burnt in the golden censer on the altar. The altar was rather small (only a cubit square), but it was relatively high (2 cubits).

The prayers and worship of the believers rise up as incense and are pleasing to God.

The daily evening burnt-offering. At this brazen altar the sacrifices were brought for the atonement of sins. Through them, sinful people found forgiveness. All these offerings pointed to the true Lamb of God.

When Christ died on the cross, the basis for every sinner's salvation was laid. The only thing that needs to be done for salvation is to turn to God, which means: to come to Him confessing all guilt. We must believe in the Lord Jesus Christ; that is, trust in the work that the Lord Jesus accomplished upon the cross.

> Would you be free from the burden of sin?
> There's power in the blood,
> Would you o'er evil a victory win?
> There's wonderful power in the blood.
>
> Would you be whiter, much whiter than snow?
> There's a power in the blood,
> Come then for cleansing to Calvary's tide;
> There's wonderful power in the blood.

The height of the altar was three cubits. We know that God has revealed Himself in three persons: God the Father, God the Son and God the Holy Spirit. Do these three Persons have anything to do with the altar, with the work of atonement? Yes, everything. The entire Godhead was involved in the salvation of man.

The Father gave His Son (1 John 4:14).
The Son gave Himself (Gal 2:20).
He offered Himself through the eternal Spirit (Heb 9:14).

In the last verse, all three Persons are mentioned; Christ, the *Son*, offered Himself without blemish to God the *Father*, through the eternal *Spirit*.

The material of the altar was wood

The altar had to be made of acacia wood. This was obtained from a tree that grew in the desert, the acacia arabica. The Lord Jesus grew up before God as a tender sapling, as a root out of dry earth (Isa 53:2; 11:1). The wood is a type of His manhood; it has grown out of the earth. We read of Him that He has been born of a woman (Gal 4:4). In Isaiah 4:2 He is called the 'fruit of the earth.'

Certainly God's Son, Jesus Christ, is the true God and eternal life (see 1 John 5:20). We ought never to forget this, for He will remain so for ever. But He, Who was and is the eternal God, came in infinite love and condescending grace to earth and became truly Man. Why did He, the almighty Creator, humble Himself so greatly? So that He *could* suffer and die (Heb 2:17). As God He could not die, could He? That was impossible. But He took part in flesh and blood; in all things He became like His brethren, though without sin, to accomplish the work of atonement for the people. He had to become Man before He could undergo the judgment of God for us. He was crucified in weakness (2 Cor 13:4). This is what the wood of the altar speaks of.

The brass

The altar gleams in the sunlight. The wood of the altar has been covered with brass. Brass typifies power (as in Job 40:18). More than that, it is a power that can withstand the fire of God's judgment. We find proof of this in Numbers 16 where we read of rebellion. There were 250 men who, in disobedience, wanted to sacrifice, but these rebels were all consumed by the fire of God's judgment (verses 35-39). But most remarkably, the brazen censers carried in their hands endured the same fire and were not consumed. The 250 lay dead, struck by lightning, but there wasn't a mark on the censers. In them was a power that could undergo the fire of God's judgment and endure it. the altar was covered with the brass of those censers.

Who had power to undergo the judgment of God? No man and no angel. Only the Righteous One, the holy Son of God. What a Person! What a Saviour! He was Man (the wood). He could endure judgment (the brass). He alone could bring the offering. He alone could accomplish the great work of redemption for which man had been waiting for forty centuries. His work is sufficient to bring the lost to God. Yes, it is sufficient to cleanse and restore all creation.

A few years ago, scientists made a discovery. A solid wooden door, covered with brass, proved to be absolutely fire resistant. This discovery was submitted to the fire department of London where it was thoroughly tested. The door withstood all tests and was certified fireproof. This shows how accurate the Bible is, it is far ahead of science.

The grating, the fire, the horns of the altar

The fire on the altar roars. Half-way up inside the altar a grating was placed, on which the wood was laid. Here the fire burned, kindled by God himself (Lev 9:24).

The man is frightened once again when the priest lays the lamb in the fire. What a blaze! 'Our God is a consuming fire,' says Hebrews 12:29.

Deeply touched, the Israelite sees the lamb, his substitute, taking his place in those flames.

I deserve the judgment. But Christ hung on the cross, enduring God's fiery wrath. It was terrible for Him. He was made sin for us, so 'that we might be made the righteousness of God in Him' (2 Cor 5:21). For three hours He was in terrible darkness, forsaken by God (Matt 27:46). Quiet worship and thanksgiving are appropriate here!

Having contemplated this love and this finished work, we can better understand why mercy cannot possibly be shown to someone who rejects the cross of Christ; why only a lake of eternal fire remains for someone who refuses to accept this Sacrifice.

The man shrinks back a few steps. Then he sees a wondrous spectacle. That great brazen altar for burnt offering ... the flames high above it ... smoke ascending to heaven ... the four horns on the corners of the altar covered with blood ... reaching toward heaven ... as if the altar were stretching its hands toward God.... The altar is presenting the sacrifice to God!

And so the altar on which the sacrifice is made has become a type of the Lord Jesus. Just as the altar has brought the offering to God, so has Christ offered Himself to God. This gave value to His offering. This wonderful Person presented it. Now we can understand Matthew 23:19. The altar is more than the offering, for the altar sanctifies the sacrifices. Christ is everything, altar and sacrifice. He is also the priest who causes the sacrifice to ascend to God in flames; He has offered up Himself.

The cross does not merely mean salvation for the sinner. There is more connected with it, something higher and more wonderful, the cross also signified the consecration of the Son to the Father.

The Son gave Himself for *us*, but in the first place He gave Himself to *God*, Who had been dishonoured by sin, and now it was His desire to glorify God. Of His own free will He underwent death to glorify God. When God as *God* hid His face from Him who was made sin, then, at the same time, the gaze of the *Father* rested full in love upon His Son. 'Therefore does My Father love me, because I lay down my life.' This He said Himself in John 10:17.

Never seated - No rest

The Israelite utters a sigh of relief. All his sins have been taken away. He can go out free. Suddenly he takes hold of the priest.

'But if I sin again tomorrow? What then?' 'Then you must come back again with another sacrifice; a goat or a sheep or a few doves.' 'And if I sin again, say next week?' 'Then you must bring yet another sacrifice! I never finish with my work here. Have you noticed that there are no chairs here? Neither in the court or in the tent itself is there a seat. There is no opportunity to sit or rest anywhere. I am not allowed to sit down at any time. I never finish. I never rest.'

The explanation for this we find in Hebrews 10:11. 'Every priest *stands* daily ministering and offering often the same sacrifices....' Why wasn't he allowed to sit in the tabernacle, in the area where he served? It was because he lived in the time of the Old Testament, and therefore, before the cross. The great work of redemption had not yet been accomplished and rest was, as yet, not possible.

Innumerable sacrifices have been brought to the slaughter. In 1 Kings 8:63 alone, we read of 22,000 bullocks and 120,000 sheep that were slain during the dedication of the temple of Solomon. Yet all these sacrifices could not take away sins. Hebrews 10:4 says, 'For it is not possible that the blood of bulls and of goats should take away sins.' Still, sins were forgiven during the old covenant, as we have just seen with the Israelite. David says in Psalm 32, 'Blessed is the man whose transgression is forgiven, whose sin is covered.'

But the forgiveness was only temporary, for when a person sinned again, he had to bring a new offering. Forgiveness was granted in view of the true sacrificial Lamb that would one day be slain on the cross (Rom 3:25).

There would be no rest; fresh sacrifices would have to be brought continually. And the result? Read Hebrews 10:11. All those sacrifices that were offered up could never take away sins.

Therefore there is no seat in the tabernacle.

A shout of triumph

Now comes the great contrast brought about by our Saviour and Redeemer. 'But this Man,' writes the apostle and explains how He after enduring the cross, 'obtained an eternal redemption', for He 'appeared to put away sin by His sacrifice of Himself' and then 'for ever sat down on the right hand of God' (Heb 9:12, 26; 10:12).

> In the past, an earthly priest — *now* the heavenly Priest.
> In the past, an animal sacrifice — *now* the Lamb of God.
> In the past, many sacrifices — *now* one sacrifice.
> In the past, repeated offerings — *now* only one.
> In the past, standing — *now* seated.
> In the past, never finished — *now* finished for ever.
> In the past, no remission of sins — *now* full remission.
> In the past, temporary forgiveness — *now* total forgiveness, for time and eternity.

Complete rest

The Lord Jesus is seated; He is now resting. He has entered into His rest (Heb 4:10). On the cross, after three hours of bitter suffering, He cried, 'It is finished!'

All has been done. Nothing remains to be done except coming to Him as a lost sinner, in all sincerity, just as you are, laying the hand on the sacrifice, acknowledging your guilt, confessing your sins. That is called 'conversion' or turning around. 'If we confess our sins, God is faithful and just to forgive us our sins and to cleanse us from all unrighteousness' (1 John 1:9). Believe in Him; trust in Him. Thank Him for this perfect redemption!

> Then doubt not thy welcome, since God has declared
> There remaineth no more to be done.
> That once in the end of the world He appeared,
> And completed the work He began.
> Look, look; look and live!
> There is life in a look at the crucified One,
> There is life at this moment for thee.

Do you know Who else is resting? God the Father. God is completely satisfied. He can rest in the work that the Son accomplished on the cross.

You may rest in the same sacrifice in which God rests.

> Sweetest rest and peace have filled us,
> Sweeter praise than tongue can tell;
> God is satisfied with Jesus,
> We are satisfied as well.

Later, when all the redeemed are above, they will not sing about themselves. They themselves are not worthy, but they will sing:

> 'Thou art Worthy … for Thou wast slain
> And hast redeemed us to God by Thy blood
> Out of every kindred, and tongue, and people, and nation;
> And hast made us unto our God kings and priests: …'
> 'Worthy is the Lamb that was slain, to receive power, and riches, and wisdom and strength, and honour and glory and blessing.' (Rev 5:9-12)

THE LAVER

Noticing another person at the laver, the Israelite asks, 'Excuse me, may I ask why that man over there is washing his hands and his feet so carefully?'

'Well, he also is a priest, as you can see by his white garment and embroidered girdle; he must wash himself before he is fit to enter the sanctuary as a purified priest. That is not meant for you; you are forbidden to enter the holy place. You are an ordinary Israelite. It is not meant for the Levites either, although they are the servants of the priests. They are only allowed to work in the court and to carry the sanctuary and its furnishings in its journeys. Only the priests may enter, for they are the sons and descendants of Aaron, the high priest. Because God is holy and they constantly defile themselves, they have strict orders to purify themselves at the laver. Otherwise they would never be able to render an undefiled service to God!'

That was the situation in the Old Testament. For this Israelite the laver was not very important. He was not allowed to pass beyond the altar. For the priest, however, the laver was important; the laver was his daily concern. And for you who are reading this, the laver is also essential, once you have accepted the Sacrifice.

We are all priests

Those who have accepted the offering are not only cleansed of their sins by God; He has also made them priests. In Revelation 1:5-6, we read that the Lord Jesus loves His own and that He made them priests unto God and His Father. Now there is a common priesthood of all believers. Every child of God is equally a priest. The New Testament does not recognize a special caste of priests, or laymen for that matter.

The Apostle Peter says to the believers to whom he writes, 'You are ... a holy priesthood to offer up spiritual sacrifices ... a royal priesthood to show forth the praises of Him who has called you' (1 Pet 2:5, 9).

Between the altar of burnt-offering and the sanctuary stood the laver, filled with water. Here the priests had to wash their hands and feet before they could enter the sanctuary. Because of their daily tasks and their path through the desert sand, they became defiled continually. To be able to continue their service before God they had to wash at the laver again and again.

So it is with each believer. Someone who has knelt at the cross is a child of God, he is also a priest. Yet, each time he becomes defiled he must return to God with confession. In this way he is repeatedly cleansed.

The four coverings of the tabernacle were placed one over the other. Here, however, they are partly pulled back to enable us to see each covering. The symbolic significance of their colours is explained in the Bible. They tell us something of the glories of Christ.

Doubt

How is it possible that many true Christians do not possess all the assurance that faith gives? They have recognized that they were guilty and lost. They have been to the altar, the cross; they have put their hand on the sacrifice. They have had moments when they trusted the words, 'the blood of Jesus Christ, His Son, cleanses us from all sin' (1 John 1:7). Perhaps they have even given thanks for their salvation. Yes, to give thanks is very important, for gratitude should automatically follow the acceptance of a gift (John 1:12,13; Col 1:12).

But all at once, everything around them became gloomy again. They saw with sorrow that they still sinned. It seemed as if they were still what they had been before. Was their conversion genuine? Doubt crept into their hearts.

Once redeemed, always saved

Must we be converted again and again? Do we need to repeat our request for redemption by the blood? Constantly stumbling and picking ourselves up again? Always uncertain? That surely is not according to God's mind. There is a misunderstanding here arising from a failure to grasp the meaning of the altar and the laver.

The altar says to an unbeliever:

You are a sinner. Through the suffering and death of Christ on the cross, the work is finished. His blood enables eternal redemption to be granted to everyone who confesses his sins and believes in Christ. The value of the work of Christ lasts for ever. This will never have to be repeated.

The laver says to a believer:

You are a child of God, but you can still be defiled by sin. These defilements must be removed after confession of guilt. For this, the Lord Jesus is our Advocate with the Father. He cleanses our feet through the washing of water by the Word. This is often repeated.

Water cleanses

The laver is the second object on the way to the sanctuary of God. It is filled with water. What is the significance of water in the Scriptures? Ephesians 5:26 says, 'He cleanses the Church with water, by the Word.' John 15:3 says, 'Ye are clean through the Word which I have spoken unto you.' Water in these passages symbolises the purifying action of the Word of God on a person.

Blood and water

After the death of Christ, a soldier pierced His side with a spear, and there came out blood and water (John 19:34). Blood speaks of atonement. Water speaks of cleansing (1 John 5:6). The blood of redemption is applied to a person at his conversion. Afterwards there is the regular repetition of the process of purification by water of which the laver reminds us.

Once we have understood the meaning of atonement and have experienced the recurring process of purification by water, the Word of God, all doubt in our life of faith will disappear.

Part *in* Him and part *with* Him

The people in the East did not wear shoes and socks, only sandals. Of course, their feet were soon dirty, especially when they sweated during the hot weather. Added to that, their roads were far more dusty than ours are. Because it wasn't permissible to lie with dirty feet on the couches around the table, it was the custom to wash the feet of the guests before a meal (Luke 7:36-50).

During the last night of His life, while the disciples were arguing about who was the greatest among them, the Lord Jesus washed the disciples' feet. He became the Servant of them all. That was too much for Peter, but the Master said, 'If I don't wash you, you have no part with Me' (John 13:8). What is significant here is the expression 'part with Me.'

Having our feet washed does not give us part in Him; that we receive at the altar, at the cross. In a practical way, in the course of our daily life, we must maintain that part— that is fellowship and contact—*with* Him.

The need for the washing of feet

A believer must always return to the laver, the Word of God. Someone who walks through the desert cannot avoid getting his feet dirty. Similarly every believer will be defiled by evil, even when we are not conscious of committing sin. The things we hear and especially the things we see in the world cause defilement in our lives. Although we may not commit an actual sin, we nevertheless need cleansing at the laver again and again.

Who washes our feet?

Although it is hard to believe, it is the Lord Jesus Himself. By means of the water, which is the Word of God, He works in His own people.

Perhaps we hear the Word or read it for ourselves. It has a power that searches us, so that we may see the wrong we have done. The Holy Scriptures are pure and perfect so that we may suddenly be led to discover that this or that must be wrong with me!

That is His way of making us recognize our wrongdoing. He leads us to repent and confess our guilt. As soon as we have confessed the wrong, we are at once forgiven. Then we are believers who have a cleansed life.

This cleansing comes about because the Lord Jesus is our Advocate with the Father. 1 John 2:1,2 says, 'My little children, these things write I unto you, that ye sin not.' This is what the Father expects from His children, though He knows that, in practice, things often turn out differently; so the verse continues that if anyone sins, his situation will not be hopeless, for we have an Advocate with the Father, Jesus Christ the Righteous.

When should we confess?

A few friends were discussing the subject of feet washing. One said, 'I have made it a habit on Saturday nights to review everything that was not right during the past few days. I confess to God and then I am able to enter the Lord's day with a happy heart.' Another said, 'No, I don't wait for Saturday night, I review all I have done every evening before I go to bed.' Then the third one explained his practice: 'Every time I do or say something that is wrong, I confess it immediately, or at least, as soon as possible. The moment a wrong thought arises, I judge it, and ban it from my heart.'

Which of these three acts according to the will of the Master? Which one benefits most from Christ's advocacy?

A child

When a child disobeys his father or mother, he still remains their child. Their relationship stems from birth and cannot be changed or undone. But a child who has been naughty cannot be happy or enjoy a close relationship to his father—there is a distance between them.

It is the same with a believer that has sinned. He remains a child of God, that is true; but he has been disobedient and thus cannot be happy. He has no liberty to pray and misses communion with the Father. To regain communion, he must confess his sin honestly before the Father. He need not come as a lost sinner to God, but rather as a child to his Father.

That is the significance of the laver. Obviously it is of great importance in the life of the believer. The laver warns him that he must walk carefully, so that he may not cause his Saviour and his Father sorrow. But whenever he has fallen and has been raised up by grace, he obtains a renewed peace and fellowship with his Redeemer defying description.

The untiring Servant

Dear brother and sister, allow Christ to wash your feet. Always confess your sins to Him to be restored to communion with Him! He is sad when you fail to do so; He rejoices when you do. For, speaking reverently, He is troubled when you are not close to Him. Open your heart wide for Him. Allow Him to remove all that hinders your peace. Won't you do so? Then there will be more power in your life, more blessing, more fruit for Him!

How inconceivably great must the love of our Saviour be! Washing our feet is not exactly a pleasant task, yet He does it again and again. On earth He was a Servant to all. He is still our Servant. He prays for us. When we are with Him in glory, He will no longer wash our feet. But even then He will continue His service. Even in heaven He will serve His own. Yes, He will do that for all eternity (see Luke 12:37).

The fulness of Christ's character is available to His own people!

The size

There is no size given for the laver. Could this be because the grace that cleanses the Christian during his walk is infinitely great? Alas, so often does a Christian go astray in his walk and sin that he loses count. But God is always prepared to remove our failures and restore us after we have confessed our wrongdoing. His love is boundless.

The women's mirrors

Where did the brass for the laver come from? In Exodus 38:8 we read that the laver was made from the mirrors of the women. They had given their mirrors for the work of God. At that time there was no glass; mirrors were made out of polished brass. To what kind of service had these mirrors been put before? The women looked at their reflection, perhaps even admiring themselves. What once had served their vanity now served a higher purpose. They gave their mirrors to God and He had them melted down to make of them a precious object for His house. A new kind of mirror was made out of them, this time to induce self-judgment and bring failure under scrutiny. In the Word of God, of which water is the type, we may examine or view ourselves in the mirror. The errors we discover in doing so can be put away, and we shall be cleansed.

The women gave their brass mirrors for His house. Have we ever given anything to God? God gave us gifts and talents. Do we keep these for ourselves? Or do we surrender them to His service? If we do so, He will make something beautiful out of them. What is given to Him, He will transform. He purifies it and uses it to His own praise and honour!

MODELS

A great number of enthusiasts have tried to build a model of the tabernacle on a reduced scale. They followed the detailed description of all materials, objects and measurements in Exodus 25-40. The model pictured in this booklet is built at a scale of 1:25 (about ¹/₂" to 1 foot) by craftsmen, in various fields, according to instructions given by the late Mr Paul F. Kiene from Switzerland. Real gold and silver were used in this model.

When we compare different models of the tabernacle, we will notice slight variations. No one knows, for instance, what form the laver had, or what the exact position was of the angels above the mercy seat. That is because we do have the specification but we lack the drawings. Moses did not need a drawing. God had shown him everything on the mountain (Ex 24).

For us, God has omitted everything that had no spiritual significance; nevertheless, He has given everything He deemed essential to convey His thoughts about His house.

THE BOARDS

Now let us examine the construction of the house. It was built of wood, of large boards. Every board was 10 cubits high (15 feet) and 1¹/₂ cubits wide (2¹/₄ feet). Altogether there were 48 of these boards. The same wood, acacia or shittim wood, was used as for the altar, so here the wood, having come out of the earth, speaks of the fact that the Lord Jesus was truly Man, born on the earth.

Gold

A tremendous amount of gold must have been required. Through the providence of God the Israelites had received it, together with other treasures, when they left Egypt (Ex 12:35-36). Inside the sanctuary the glittering gold must have been a beautiful and awesome sight!

The most precious metal, gold, can be found throughout the Bible, starting with Genesis 2, in the garden of Eden. Throughout history, gold has been desired more than anything else. Even in Revelation 21, we find an abundance of gold in the description of the New Jerusalem. This city is described as having the glory of God, and is of pure gold. Even its street was of pure gold. Gold speaks of heaven, of God's glory.

The wood of the boards portrays Christ's true humanity, the gold His divine glory. In His walk on earth He was God and Man in one Person, God revealed in the flesh (1 Tim 3:16). At first sight people beheld His humanity; only a few discovered the gold, His divine glory. To the Father, it was the very opposite: just as with the boards of this house, so He saw first the gold, the Godhead of His Son. But the Father's eye penetrated deeper: concealed within lay His true humanity.

A Christian also resembles such a wooden board; he is man on earth. But he is, as it were, overlaid with gold. This is certainly a great wonder, but the Bible says that every believer, every child of God, is clothed with the righteousness of God (2 Cor 5:21). Just as the lost, prodigal son in Luke 15 received the best robe from his father, so every believer can say: 'My soul praises God, for He has clothed me with the garments of salvation, He has covered me with the robe of righteousness' (Isa 61:10).

Just as the gold covered the boards, the believer is 'a man in Christ' (2 Cor 12:2); consequently, he is clothed with heavenly glory.

God dwelt in Christ

In the time of the people of Israel, the boards covered with gold formed the walls of the tabernacle. Here was the place where God dwelt. Later, the Son of God came to earth. Then God dwelt in Him, in the Lord Jesus. 'That in Him should all fulness dwell' (Col 1:19).

God dwelling in every believer

Now that Christ has been received up into heaven, every believer is a dwelling place, a temple in which God the Holy Spirit resides. 'Do ye not know that your body is the temple of the Holy Spirit, which is in you, which ye have of God ... ?' (1 Cor 6:19).

God dwelling in the church

These boards standing shoulder to shoulder, as it were, formed God's dwelling upon the earth. In the same way there is a dwelling of God in our day. It is God's purpose that all believers, joined together, should form the house in which God dwells today. Now He no longer dwells in a material house of gold, nor in a stone temple as in the days of Solomon.

The house of God is the church of the living God, as it says in 1 Timothy 3:15, while Ephesians 2:22 teaches that believers are built for a habitation of God in the Spirit. That is clear enough! 'Whose house are we,' are the words written to the Hebrews (Heb 3:6). The believers in the New Testament formed the House of God, just as all believers do today.

All true children of God together form the church of Christ. They (as Peter expresses it in chapter 2 of his first epistle), 'as living stones, are being built up a spiritual house, a holy priesthood.'

The truth is still practicable!

What a pity that believers no longer stand shoulder to shoulder like the boards, that factions and divisions occur among Christians. For a short time after the beginning of the church, the unity was still evident. It was said to the Corinthians, 'You are the temple of the living God, according as God has said: 'I will dwell among them...' (2 Cor 6:16).

Nevertheless, it is possible to feel in our hearts this unity of all true believers, this oneness of all true children of God. It is possible to come together on the basis of this unity. This can be realized and experienced even today. Would He, Who established every single detail of the earthly worship of Israel, not guide His children in our time, too? Most certainly He would! But where shall we find this guidance? Where else than in His Word?

When we, in accordance with the Word, separate ourselves from unbelievers (2 Cor 6:17) and join those who call upon the Lord out of a pure heart (2 Tim 2:19-22), then we may come together unto the Name of the Lord Jesus. To gather in, or unto, His Name is to gather around Himself. Then the Lord Jesus is the Centre. He leads. He has the authority. He alone has the right to set the rules. He alone presides. Those who meet in this way have His promise, made in Matthew 18:20, that He will be in their midst.

Were all those boards unconnected?   Exodus 26:26-29

Most certainly not. As the staves of a barrel are kept together by the hoops, so there were four bars, inserted through golden rings, holding the boards together and keeping them standing.

In the beginning, when the church had only recently been formed (Acts 2), there were also four things that held it together. Verse 42 says that they continued with perseverance in:

the apostle's doctrine,
the fellowship,
the breaking of bread,
and prayer.

Besides these, there was a bar that could not be seen from the outside; it ran through the centre of the boards. That bar resembles love, which is the bond of perfection (Col 3:14).

The foundation

Exodus 26:19-25

The foundation of the house of Gold certainly had to be quite sturdy, for it stood simply in the desert sand. The most important thing in the building of a house is the base, the foundation. It must be solid.

The divine Architect had determined that the footings of His house would consist of large blocks of silver, every block weighing about 90 pounds. Two blocks were placed under each board. Every board had two tenons or pins at its lower end, and in each block of silver was a hole. Each of the pins fitted in one of the holes in the silver foundation. What a costly foundation!

The silver

Exodus 30:11-16; 38:25-28

Where did all the silver come from? God had told Moses to count the people, all the men from twenty to fifty years of age. But everyone who was included in this reckoning had to pay a price. It was called the atonement money, or the atonement silver. The price of atonement was the same for everyone, whether rich or poor, half a shekel of silver. This principle has remained, even in our days: a person is only counted among the true people of God, as belonging to the church of the Lord Jesus Christ, when the price of atonement has been paid for him or her.

The footings of the tabernacle were made of that silver. For each of the 48 boards there were two bases. The entire house of God and each individual board thus rested on the price of atonement that had been paid.

Throughout the whole Bible silver is used as a means of payment. Abraham bought a field for 400 pieces of silver; Joseph, a young man, was sold for 20 pieces of silver; Judas sold his Master for 30 pieces of silver. Some languages have the same word for silver and money. The Bible uses silver as a type of the *price* Christ paid for atonement. That price was His precious blood. What a costly price!

The house of God is established in our days on the selfsame basis: the price of atonement, the high price that our Redeemer paid for the atonement. Such thoughts, which have come to fruition in the church, and which were incorporated in this wonderful House of Gold, can only be of divine origin.

We are not redeemed, or purchased, by silver or gold, but by the precious blood of Christ, as of a Lamb without blemish and without spot (1 Pet 1:18-19).

THE CLOUD

A *cloud rested* on the tabernacle above the place where the ark stood. This cloud indicated that God was present. It also functioned as a guide while the people of God journeyed (Ex 40:36-38). When the cloud lifted from over the tabernacle, the building had to be taken down in accordance with Numbers 4. The entire nation had to be put into its ranks, ready for departure. They then proceeded. Where to? In the direction that God indicated by means of the cloud. God was their Guide. How far did they have to go? To the place where the cloud stopped. Then the tabernacle had to be set up again and the cloud again rested on the dwelling. In Numbers 9:15-23 we find a vivid description of this (see also chapter 10:33-36).

What about us? We have no pillar of cloud. Yet as long as we are in the world, which is a desert for the Christian, we have a good Leader. Not in the form of a visible cloud, but in the

Holy Spirit, Who dwells in us. Everyone who *has come* to God with his sins *and believes* in the finished work of the Lord Jesus Christ has this divine Guest dwelling within him. Ephesians 1:3-13 and 1 Corinthians 6:19 confirm this.

The Holy Spirit leads believers when they express their dependence in prayer. Whoever says: 'I don't know the way; Lord, lead me, be my Guide,' will be led safely and will be kept from straying from the path. 'I will instruct you and teach you the way in which you shall go: I will counsel you with mine eye upon you.' (Psalm 32:8).

FOUR COLOURS

The curtains of the tabernacle were all woven and embroidered in the four following colours: white, blue, purple, scarlet.

Let us have a closer look at these colours and try to discover what the Bible says about them. In doing this we shall notice that they tell us all kinds of things about the Lord Jesus. Could it be otherwise? He has many glories and the subject of the tabernacle reflects many facets of His beauty. God the Father knows Him fully (Matt 11:27). It is the Father's pleasure to show His children something of the treasures that are hidden in His beloved Son.

In the four gospels four different aspects of the Lord's character are described. We shall find these characters in the colours of the tabernacle.

White linen

The first colour is white. The white linen speaks of purity and righteousness.

Think of the great white throne in Revelation 20 and the pure, fine linen, signifying the righteousness of the saints in Revelation 19:8. The white in the curtains stands for the purity of Christ. In the linen we see His pure and perfect life, always rendering service to God and men. He was the perfect Man and faithful Servant. In the gospel of *Mark* especially He is portrayed in this light.

When the coverings are taken away, we look inside the holy place. The walls, 10 cubits high, were covered with gold. The first thing we notice is the curtain of the holy place. Then we see the golden candlestick spreading its light. To the right stands the table with the loaves of bread. Further back is the golden altar for the burning of incense. Beyond this hangs the veil of the holy of holies. This veil was embroidered with cherubim. Beyond this last veil was the holy of holies or the most holy place with the ark, where God dwelt. There the priests performed their service. No one was allowed to enter the holy of holies except the high priest once a year on the day of atonement.

In our times things are entirely different. When the Lord Jesus died, the veil was rent and the way to God was opened!

On the golden table were twelve loaves of showbread. Every loaf represented a tribe of Israel. The entire nation was on display, so to speak, before God. He sees his own in the heavenly light of the candlestick. Around the table the golden border symbolized the entire nation united and protected.

In the background you will notice a vessel for wine. Bowls have been placed on the loaves. (Ex 25:29 mentions these although not stating where they were placed).

Blue

It is not very difficult to understand the meaning of the blue. Just look up to heaven. Christ is called the Lord from heaven (1 Cor 15:47), the Lord of glory (1 Cor 2:8). During His walk on earth He was 'the One who comes from heaven' (John 3:31); indeed 'the One who is in heaven' (John 3:13).

He became Man, but He remained the Son of God; He is God the Son. Jesus Christ is the true God and eternal life (1 John 5:20). As God the Son we learn to know Him in the gospel of *John*.

Purple

This was a very costly material, worn only by kings and rich people. It is remarkable that in the Scriptures purple is seen practically only outside the country of Israel, and more particularly in the courts of the great empires.*)

Purple stands for universal riches. It is connected with the glory of the Lord Jesus as Son of Man, as seen in Psalm 8, where everything is put under His feet. This is how we see Him in the gospel of Luke: The Son of Man, but, even in suffering and death, Lord of lords and King of kings.

---

*) In Judges 8:26 the kings of the Midianites had purple coats. Other lands that are connected with purple are: Tyre, 2 Chron 2:13-14; Persia, Esther 1:6; 8:15; Elisha, i.e. Javan or Greece, Ezek 27:7; 1 Chron 1:7; Syria, Ezek 27:16; Babylon, Dan 5:29. All those countries form a wide circle around Israel.

Scarlet, in contrast to purple, occurs in Scripture only in connection with Israel. It also was precious. The Lord Jesus will possess this greatness and royal glory as King of Israel. Only in Matthew 27:28 do we see Him with a scarlet robe. His kingship over Israel is the great theme of the gospel of *Matthew*.

Remarkably, many thousands of snails and worms give their lives in the production of blue, purple and scarlet dyes. In these colours is, therefore, something that reminds us of the death of the sacrificial animals.

THREE ENTRANCES

The gate in the curtains around the court was the first entrance. Through this curtain one entered into the court.

The second entrance was closed off by the curtain of the holy place. Through this only the priests were allowed to enter when they performed their services.

The third entrance was the veil that closed off the holy of holies. Even the priest was not allowed to enter there. Only the high priest was allowed to go in once a year, on the day of atonement.

All three curtains were woven in the above mentioned colours. Only the third one, the veil before the holy of holies, portrayed cherubim as well. This signified that these holy beings always guard the glory of God. Behind this veil was the ark, where God dwelt.

The first curtain, the gate to the court, was 20 cubits wide and 5 cubits high. The two curtains of the holy place were 10 cubits wide and 10 cubits high. The first one was exceptionally wide, the others were narrower and higher. Let us see what this might mean.

Free entry

At the first door, God invites sinners and, happily, many enter. They become redeemed sinners, who are for ever blessed. As we saw when we spoke of the laver, instead of sinners, they are now priests. Nowadays, from the time of the New Testament, they are allowed to go further, even into the heavenly sanctuary itself.

But how unfortunate that many go no further than the altar. Do they find the veil too narrow, too high, too sacred? Won't they venture further? They could proceed and enjoy much more, but they don't. This is sad! They miss the privilege of entering step by step into the House of Gold.

But should we not wait to enter heaven till we are called away from the earth? As far as our bodies are concerned this is true, but even *now* every Christian has the great privilege of entering into the presence of God as a priest to offer up spiritual sacrifices of praise and worship.

He is actually allowed to do what was previously prohibited to the priests: he may enter through the third, the last veil and proceed into the holy of holies, the inner sanctuary, into the immediate presence of the throne of God.

When the Saviour died on the cross, the veil of the holy of holies in the temple was rent in two, from the top to the bottom. This was God's doing. It wasn't the work of men, for it was rent *from* the top *to* the bottom. The death of Christ opened the way to the glory of God.

We possess full liberty to enter into the sanctuary through the veil. (Heb 10:19-20) This privilege is *yours* as well as mine, brother and sister in Christ. Let us boldly make use of it!

> The veil is rent: our souls draw near
> Unto the throne of grace.
> The merits of the Lord appear,
> They fill the holy place.

THE TENT CURTAINS

The boards for the walls and the pillars from which the curtains were hanging might be called the frame of the building. Over this frame, four large tent curtains were spread; together they formed the roof of the building. They protected the House of Gold and safeguarded it against wind and weather.

Anyone standing in the holy place or in the holy of holies and looking up, would be filled with admiration. It would be like looking straight into heaven. There he would see a beautiful large curtain in the four colours, covered with cherubim, as if to inform him: The Holy One dwells here! This was the lowest of four curtains that covered the entire tabernacle. It was 40 by 28 cubits. Over it lay the second curtain of goats' hair. This was 44 by 30 cubits, larger than the lowest curtain, and was called 'the tent over the tabernacle.'

This 'tent' protected the beautiful lowest curtain and served additionally as a safeguard, separating the entire building from its surroundings. Symbolically these covering curtains, especially this second one, signify separation. This means the House of God has been separated or set apart from the world and from all that is not fit for the presence of God. True believers, built together for an habitation of God must be characterised by this same feature.

We should observe that separation is not strictness towards unbelievers, but rather towards ourselves, that we may be separated from evil. Christ's walk manifested this perfectly when he was on earth.

Red-dyed rams' skins formed the third covering. A ram was slain during the consecration service for the priests, at the time of their sanctification for the service of God (Ex 29:15-35; Lev 8:2). This sacrificial animal stands for the absolute consecration of the Son to the Father: obedient unto death on the cross! (Phil 2:8) Dyed red strengthens the thought of His death and the shedding of His blood.

The outer covering was made of badgers' skins. From the outside these skins look very unattractive. Someone that has not repented cannot appreciate Christ. But everyone who has come to know Him will be aware that he is safe and sheltered. Outward influences could never touch this covering. So with Christ, the unchangeable One, sin could not touch Him.

Christ could withstand every temptation and all opposition. Under His care we are safe, and are kept in fellowship with Him.

CO-WORKERS WANTED! Exodus 31:1 -11

It must have required great skill and craftsmanship to build this structure! Woodwork, embroidery, metalwork etc. ....

The two men called by God and put in charge of this work were Bezaleel (the name means 'under God's shadow') and Aholiab (his name means 'my tent is the Father'). In Scripture, the character of persons is often expressed by their name. Their names indicated that Bezaleel and Aholiab lived in close communion with God.

Of Bezaleel we read: 'I have filled him with the Spirit of God' (Ex 31:3). Aholiab was not the only one to help. In Exodus 31:6 God says: 'In the hearts of all that are wise hearted I have put wisdom, that they may make all that I have commanded thee.'

So it is today; every one may be filled with God's Spirit (Eph 5:18) and be granted wisdom (James 1:5), so that he can help in the building of the House of God on earth (1 Cor 3:10-15; 1 Pet 2:5).

Every Israelite could bring building materials and gifts, and so contribute to the work (Ex 25:1-9; 35:20-24). We may do more than that. We may give not just our possessions, but ourselves, our entire lives. We may give, not out of necessity, but with a free will. Our God is worthy of it a thousand times over. Moreover, what we keep for ourselves, we must soon leave behind — we shall lose it; what we give to Him is profit — and remains ours for ever!

The women

Who wove and embroidered those curtains and coverings? That must have been a tremendous undertaking! This great work was certainly done by the women. Women were not allowed to do the work of the priest in the tabernacle, not even the service of the Levite. But God had a special task for their sensitive fingers: to prepare the covering, the exterior of His dwelling. Has not this service remained unchanged?

Even today the faithful woman has the delicate task of being specially responsible for the clothing, the covering of God's people in whose midst He dwells. She has the care not just for her own appearance, but for that of the entire family. It begins with the children. Does she, by means of their clothing, teach them modesty? It is especially the mother who influences the way the children's taste in clothing and appearance develops and generally it is the mother in the final instance who determines the father's appearance: whether the entire family is dressed according to God's thoughts is ultimately her decision. What a task for the woman to persevere lovingly in embroidering the covering of God's dwelling, the assembly!

Just as the women of Israel wove the coverings that symbolize the glory of Christ, so a sister in Christ, by her behaviour, her attitude, her words, and the influence she has, can show a little of what the Lord Jesus means to her.

THE HOLY PLACE

What were the objects in the holy place? The candlestick, the table of showbread and the altar of incense.

The candlestick

Exodus 25:31-40

What is the first thing I see in the holy place? The light, the candlestick. God is light. Christ was the light of the world (John 9:5). The candlestick was of pure gold, not simply cast, but forged out of one talent of gold, by an able goldsmith with a hammer. That pure gold was beaten and beaten and beaten yet again. He who is the true light suffered and was beaten with the severe blows of God's judgment.

The shaft of the candlestick with the six arms or branches formed a whole. The seven oil lamps that were on it gave light in the darkness. The lamps were filled with olive oil, which is a type of the Holy Spirit (Zech 4:1-6). So it is with believers who are closely connected with Christ: they can spread light as well, but they can only do so by the Holy Spirit.

Every lamp was separately cared for. The burned part of the wick gave no light, so first the priest had to remove it. A believer whose life is clogged by uncleanness does not spread light. A pair of snuffers must be applied; these snuffers were also of gold. That was a delicate task, but in the end the light shone again in all its brilliance. This light had to fall first of all on the shaft of the candlestick, on Christ. That is the meaning of Numbers 8:2,3.

Let us keep in mind that the light we give should not fall on us, but on the Lord Jesus. He must be placed in the light, He must be glorified!

Later, in heaven, He will again be the Light: 'The street of the city was pure gold ... and the city had no need of the sun, neither of the moon, to shine in it: for the glory of God did lighten it, and the Lamb (Christ) is the light thereof' (Rev 21:21,23).

Opposite the candlestick stood the golden table, on which lay twelve loaves of bread, exactly the same as the number of tribes in Israel.

The table is Christ (remember the wood with the gold). Just as the table bore the loaves of bread, so Christ bears God's people *today*. They are acceptable to God, because *He* bears them. God sees them in the light of the heavenly candlestick. The twelve loaves of bread signify the *entire* nation of Israel. When the ten tribes were carried away to Assyria and only two remained in the land, there remained twelve loaves on the table.

That is how we must see the twelve loaves in our day, too. It means that our heart, our love, and our prayers should embrace the entire people of God. There is division: groups and sects prevail. To our shame we must humbly acknowledge this. But among them we find God's children everywhere. There is unity. God knows His own, so let us hold out our hand to them as brethren and love them wholeheartedly.

> Father ... I pray for them ...
> which Thou hast given me, ...
> that they may be one,
> as We are ... (John 17:9-11).

Surrounding the table was a golden border, a hand's breadth, forming a golden enclosure. No doubt this served to prevent the loaves from failing or sliding off the table.

The Lord Jesus is this golden border. The border was one hand's breadth. The hand of the Lord Jesus maintains a firm grip on His own. He protects them. Are not the hands of the Son of God enough to hold His own?

The bread

Every Sabbath the loaves of bread were eaten by the priests and replaced by new loaves. The bread on the golden table was food for the priests. God had so ordered it. John 6:32-58 says that the Lord Jesus is the living bread that came down out of heaven, and that if anyone eats

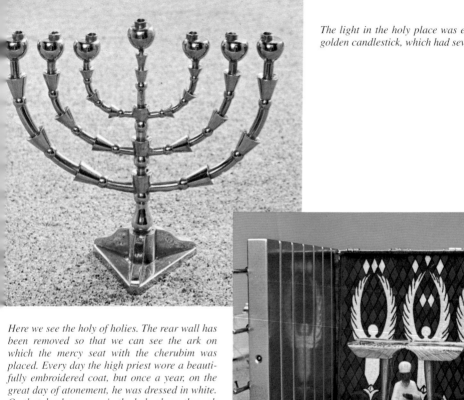

The light in the holy place was emitted by the golden candlestick, which had seven oil lamps.

Here we see the holy of holies. The rear wall has been removed so that we can see the ark on which the mercy seat with the cherubim was placed. Every day the high priest wore a beautifully embroidered coat, but once a year, on the great day of atonement, he was dressed in white. On that day he came, via the holy place, through the veil which gave entrance to the holy of holies.

This veil can be clearly seen in this picture. The veil was rent when the Lord Jesus died, and in this way access to the throne of God was provided for us.

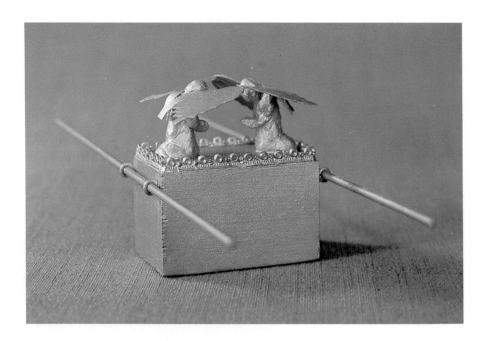

The ark of the covenant was covered within and without with gold. God is so great that even the heaven of heavens cannot contain Him, yet in condescending love He placed His throne here.

On the ark lay a plate of pure gold, $2^1/_2$ by $1^1/_2$ cubits, which was the mercy seat. From the two ends of the mercy seat rose two cherubim of gold which were formed out of the same piece. The faces of the cherubim were turned to the blood that the high priest had sprinkled on the mercy seat, which spoke of atonement.

Through this blood the throne of the thrice-holy God, which ought to have been a throne of judgment, had become a throne of grace. For us the significance is that the sinner can only come to God because God sees the blood: the finished work of His well-beloved Son on the cross.

of this bread, he will live forever.

The life of the Christian is fed by the true Bread. Feeding upon Him, being occupied with Him through His Word, receiving Him and enjoying Him gives spiritual growth and true blessing.

The golden altar of incense

Exodus 30:1-9

The golden altar of incense was not used to offer animals for sacrifice as was the great brazen altar in the court. Only sweet-smelling incense could be burnt here. The pleasant odour of the incense rose up to God. What this symbolizes becomes clear when we read Psalm 141:2 and Revelation 8:3.

Incense speaks of the prayers of the saints (the believers), but it also signifies thanksgiving, praise and worship of the people of God, as we can see from Hebrews 13:15. It all ascends to God, but it is brought upon the altar. The altar, as it were, brings it to God. So Christ brings our prayers and thanksgiving to God. Could they be acceptable to God if they came directly from us? No, Christ purifies and sanctifies them.

In this way every believer may approach God as a priest, but besides this, all the children of God together, as a holy priesthood, may offer up spiritual sacrifices acceptable to God through Jesus Christ (1 Pet 2:5-9).

> To Him that loves us, gave Himself,
> And died to do us good;
> Has washed us from our scarlet sins
> In His most precious blood;
> Who made us kings and priests to God,
> His Father infinite;
> To Him eternal glory be,

And everlasting might.

Through Him to God, the God most high
Praise for all grace be given;
Whose gifts through all eternity
We'll gladly sing in heaven;
His Christ has loved us, given Himself,
And died to do us good,
Has washed us from our scarlet sins
In His own precious blood.

Rest

A sparrow and a swallow have their nest, a refuge where they can rest (Psalm 84:3). Then the Psalmist continues to describe that place of rest as being at 'Thine altars, O Lord of Hosts, my King, and my God.' *Altars* it says, in the plural, for there are two.

A person must first of all find rest at the brazen altar of burnt-offering that is in the court. This means he must find atonement at the cross. There is the start of his life of faith. Later he finds rest at the golden altar of incense, through prayer and worship.

Worship is the highest thing a man can give. It begins on earth and will never end. Here we may begin to offer up praise and worship, but it will remain our task in heaven throughout all eternity (Rev 5).

The Incense

Incense had to be compounded, but only according to accurate and divine instructions laid down in Exodus 30:34-38. It was to be made with four components. No one was allowed to copy it or to smell it. The fragrance of the Incense was a secret for God alone, just as the full enjoyment of the glory of the well-beloved Son belongs only to the Father.

The Father always regards the Son with full affection.

> 'This is My beloved Son...
> in Whom I am well pleased...'

While considering the burnt-offering we saw the work of redemption that Christ accomplished. In the incense we see what He is in Himself. Here it is not a question of what He has done or accomplished; no matter how great that may be, but of His personal qualities. A person is more than the work he has done. We think of His greatness, His wonderful love and His many other glories.

May we, as priests, offer this up to God? Yes, we may bring to the Father all that we have found and admired in the Son. We can rejoice in all that we have found in the Lord Jesus, all that we have enjoyed in His Person, and we may talk about that with the Father. In this way we may have fellowship with the Father and the Son.

Of course, it remains true that we shall never be able to give sufficient thanks for the accomplished redemption and for the blessing that we have received from it. But incense, worship, is more than thanksgiving: it is enjoying what the Son is, His beauty, His love, and all His personal riches with the Father. This is a sweet-smelling savour to the Father.

My brother and sister, do you love the Lord Jesus? When you meditate on the Lord Jesus, how great, how full of love He is, then you may approach God and tell Him this: that is worship. That is pouring out the spikenard ointment of our soul, as Mary of Bethany did when she anointed His feet and the house was filled with the odour of the ointment (John 12).

That is offering sweet smelling incense.

The Floor

What did the floor of the house consist of? You might expect it to be of the same material as the walls, of gold. Or perhaps you might think, of wood. Both thoughts are wrong; the floor was sand. How can that be? The House of God, in all its splendour and beauty, set apart for

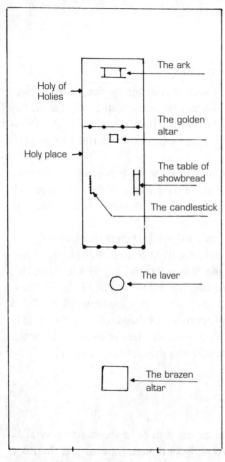

Plan of the Tabernacle

the highest Majesty, yet it has an earthen floor? Yes, the House of God with all those golden objects stood on the sand.

For us this means that God's people are on a journey, through a desert that has nothing to offer to the Christian's new life. The caravan moves on. There are difficulties; there is sadness and disappointment, sickness and death around us. But we are not alone. Every day God is with us in the desert. He does not loose sight of His people. What love! What a tremendous help! Even in your difficulties, He is close to you. 'All power is given unto Me in heaven and in earth ... and lo, I am with you alway.' (Matt 28:18-20).

Be brave a little longer, for He is with us. Soon the goal will be reached, and we shall be with Him!

The Poles

The poles for bearing the table and the ark mean the same thing; the objects of the House of God were to be carried. God was journeying with His people. But the poles also have something to tell us about our task. The Levites carried these costly objects that speak of Christ. Everyone who met them in the wilderness could see that they were carrying precious treasures.

Today we believers also carry wonderful things along with us. We show others who He is and what we possess in Him. In this way we may witness of Him, so that sinners may be saved. But are we doing this? Are the poles on our shoulders?

If today people know about the redeeming love of God, it is only through us. God only uses redeemed sinners to spread the gospel. Let us do our share of the work!

THE HIGH PRIEST Exodus 28

Anyone who has seen the high priest, or rather, everyone who has seen his clothing and understands what these clothes have to say about the heavenly High Priest; will sense a deep-seated gratitude, and can live happily, with an unshakeable trust.

The ephod

First let us look at the ephod, the top garment of the high priest. Once again we notice the embroidery in the four well-known colours. But notice! Threads of gold have been worked through it (Ex 39:3). We saw that gold speaks of heavenly glory. Indeed, the Lord Jesus is now our High Priest in heaven.

He *was* on earth. He *knows* what it means to live here. He knows our difficulties and sorrows, like no one else. Now He can sympathise with us, and that is just what He does. He understands everything about you and me. He helps His own. He is the merciful High Priest (Heb 4:15).

The stones set in the shoulder-plates

What about these stones on the right and on the left shoulders of the high priest? They are precious stones. Six names are engraved on each stone, twelve in all, the number of the tribes of Israel. The entire nation was carried on the shoulders of the high priest.

Today the Lord Jesus carries all who belong to Him, all the people of God, on His strong shoulders, just as the good shepherd carries the lamb on his shoulders, bringing it home.

The breastplate

The breastplate was square, and also embroidered with gold. On it were twelve different, sparkling, precious stones, set in gold, with the names of the twelve tribes engraved in them. Precious stones are the most beautiful products of the earth and often they have an immense value. Here, unlike those on the shoulders, every name is engraved in a separate precious stone. The former were of the same type, but here we have twelve different stones. Those symbolised the nation as a whole; these have each name engraved in a separate stone.

That gives us two reasons to rejoice: the Lord Jesus upholds the church as a whole (the shoulders); He knows us individually (the breastplate). Once you are saved, your name is known in heaven. The Lord Jesus values you as a precious jewel. Our value does not derive from ourselves, but from Him. He then carries you on His loving heart.

This does not apply to unbelievers. In Scripture their name has no value for God. Think of the rich man's story in Luke 16. His name is not mentioned. But Lazarus' name is known; his name means 'God is my Helper.' On earth he was unknown, but he was well known in heaven.

The names of the believers are engraved; they can never be erased. They shine in the light of heaven. The brighter the light, the more they sparkle. Everything has come by grace and all is made possible by the High Priest. We are all on His shoulders together—borne by His power, separate on His heart—borne by His love.

The high priest in his ornate garments.

The ephod, a kind of apron, was in the four colours: blue, purple, scarlet, and white linen, all interwoven with gold.

Here we have a beautiful type of Christ in His office of High Priest for His own. He rose from among the dead, ascended to heaven and is seated at God's right hand. As a merciful and compassionate High Priest, He ever lives and prays for His own to help them in their difficulties. He carries the names of His redeemed ones on His strong shoulders; besides that, the name of each of His own is engraved in a stone of the breast plate and thus is carried on His loving heart.

After the entire building with its precious objects had been made according to God's design, His glory came to dwell in the House of God. His presence was visible by the pillar of cloud that rested on the sanctuary, above the place where the ark stood. Here we get a solemn impression of the holiness of God that required judgment upon the sinner. Look however at the fire upon the altar! God executed that judgment upon the Lamb that He Himself had provided: His beloved Son.

Now the way to God is open for everyone who wants to come. Outside of Him there is no life but eternal destruction. With Him, in His house above, there is infinite glory. A friendly invitation to come there is extended to everyone.

O God we come with singing,
Because Thy great High Priest
Our names to Thee is bringing,
Nor e'er forgets the least:
For us He wears the mitre,
Where 'Holiness' shines bright;
For us His robes are whiter
Than heaven's unsullied light.

Wherefore, holy brethren, partakers of the heavenly calling, consider the Apostle and High Priest of our profession, Christ Jesus (Heb 3). He ever lives to make intercession for us. We need such a High Priest (Heb 7).

Urim and Thummim

The breastplate is folded double. Why? Because something was hidden in it; it contained the Urim and the Thummim. Most likely these were jewels; their names mean 'lights and perfections'.

When someone had to make an important decision but did not know exactly what God wanted him to do, he went to the high priest. The priest was able to tell, by means of the Urim and Thummim, what God's will was. Through them God gave His answer, and the enquirer obtained perfect light on how to act.

Perhaps someone thinks, 'I wish we had a high priest who could always show us the way!' Well, that is exactly what we have, though fortunately not on earth, where we might have to travel a long distance to get help! Our High Priest is in heaven, and by means of prayer we have a direct connection with Him.

We can approach our High Priest with every problem. He is there for us. He lives for His own. He doesn't leave us in doubt. We can tell Him everything, and then we must wait quietly for His answer. In His time He will make the path clear to us.

The robe

The robe of the ephod was made entirely of blue. Pomegranates in three colours, alternating with golden bells, were attached to the lower hem.

When we think of this, we recognize its beauty, for the bells make a sound. But sound alone, mere talk, is not enough. That explains the alternation of bells and pomegranates. The amount of sound equalled the amount of fruit: words and works were there in equal measure.

With Christ we find those things in perfect balance (Luke 24: 19).

The mitre

Upon the forehead of the high priest, attached to the mitre or headgear of fine woven linen, was a golden plate on which was engraved: HOLINESS TO THE LORD.

The people of God in themselves were unworthy. But God saw that plate of gold with its inscription, and so Israel was sanctified. In our time God's people are also sanctified and acceptable to God, but only in and through the Lord Jesus, our great High Priest.

> ...that 'we might have a strong consolation, who have fled for refuge to lay hold upon the hope set before us: which hope we have as an anchor of the soul, both sure and steadfast, and which enters into that within the veil; whither the forerunner is for us entered, even Jesus, made a High Priest for ever.' (Heb 6:18-20).

THE HOLY OF HOLIES

The ark

Finally we may enter the holy of holies. What do we find there? In that perfect space, symbolized by its cubic measure of 10 x 10 x 10 cubits, everything was of gold. There the ark, the throne of God, stood behind the veil. That was the place where God dwelt.

The ark was a wooden box, covered on the inside and on the outside with pure gold. From this we see that the ark was a type of Christ. On the ark lay a large golden plate, the mercy-seat, $2^1/_2$ by $1^1/_2$ cubits, with the golden cherubim over it. Here God dwelt, approachable in dazzling light. That light was surrounded by dark clouds. 'There shall no man see Me, and live.' (Ex 33:20)

It is a good thing that we do not live under the law, but in the age of grace (Rom 6:14).

Those who belong to Christ may now contemplate the glory of the Lord with uncovered faces (2 Cor 3:18).

What was in the ark?

The things kept in the ark give us further evidence that the ark was a type of Christ.

There were the tablets with the law, the ten commandments. Only Christ could say to God, when He was on earth: 'Thy law is within My heart.' (Psalm 40:8) The Lord Jesus carried the law of God in His heart.

Then there was the golden pot with manna in the ark. According to John 6, Christ is the true Manna, the food for the pilgrim's journey. The holy of holies is a type of heaven; there we no longer need the manna. But why then do we find the manna here? There above, it will serve as a heavenly reminder of all the enjoyment that we had from Christ even when we were on earth.

Finally, we find in the ark Aaron's almond rod that budded (Num 17). The almond tree flowers earlier than any other tree and it speaks of new life after the winter when all is dead. The staff is, therefore, connected with the resurrection, with Christ as the risen Victor, our Living High Priest.

The mercy seat

The mercy seat covered the ark. Here was the throne of God; it was of pure gold. Here dwelt the thrice-holy One, the Almighty. This throne should have been a throne of judgment. The law, transgressed by Israel, lay beneath it. God dwelt in the midst of a sinful people. Actually He should have destroyed them, done away with them for ever. But once a year, the high priest sprinkled blood on the seat. That blood spoke of the perfect Sacrifice. By means of this blood the throne of judgment was changed into a throne of grace (Rom 3:25).

The cherubim

Cherubim are exalted beings. They guard the throne of God. Cherubim with drawn swords barred the way to the garden of Eden (Gen 3). But in the tabernacle they are connected with grace. Their wings were spread over the mercy seat. Their faces looked down, as if in admiration, at the blood that was sprinkled upon it (Lev 16).

The throne

The great High Priest, our Lord Jesus, has, by His own blood, entered once for all into the holy of holies, having obtained an eternal redemption (Heb 9:12; 4:16). Now there is not a throne of judgment in heaven, but a throne of grace. Whoever comes to the throne to receive mercy and blessing now is a happy person indeed. The time for grace has already lasted a good 1900 years; it is approaching its end.

At Christ's return the time of judgment will begin. Then the time of grace is past for you and you can no longer be saved. Then it will be too late, and you and all those that have not repented, will face another throne: the throne of judgment.

In Revelation 20:11-15 we see the dead, great and small, standing before the great white Throne; no one will be acquitted there. All that do not come to the throne of grace will stand before that terrible, majestic throne. They will hear the sentence and will have to agree: 'Because of my sins I deserve this judgment. On earth I did not want to be saved; now I shall be cast for ever into the lake of fire burning with brimstone. It isn't God's fault that I am lost. He was full of love and He wanted to save me, but I didn't want to be saved.'

What endless remorse there will be: crying and gnashing of teeth! 'If I had only listened. I was so close, but now I am in outer darkness.'

It is more than *our* earnest prayer; it is *God's* earnest desire that you who are reading this booklet will become happy for time and eternity!

HOUSE OF GOD, WELCOME!

We are outside, far from God. We are sinners, enemies. We had a great debt and deserved to stay outside in our misery, in outer darkness, in eternal night.

We entered through the open door. The Lord Jesus was that Door. At the altar we saw God's love for us, which caused His only Son to be slain on the cross. There we found reconciliation and peace with God. So we came to the House of Gold.

It surpassed all our expectations. We saw the riches of the Lord Jesus in the candlestick, the table and the golden altar. Through the veil we came into the heavenly light that surrounded the throne of God. There is our home. God wants to have lost sinners there. Is this a dream? No, it is reality! Now we see it by faith, but soon we shall see it in reality.

What love God revealed! How great is His grace! How wonderful is the Person Who has accomplished all this, the Son of God! None can be compared to Him! 'He Who testifies these things says, Surely I come quickly' (Rev 22).

When He has come to take His own to His home above, the eternal song of praise of the numberless redeemed ones will sound through the halls of heaven. It will be a mighty choir, the singing will be with perfect voices, accompanied by perfect music:

'Unto Him that loved us, and washed us from our sins in His own blood, and has made us kings and priests unto God and His Father; to Him be glory and dominion for ever and ever. Amen.'

Will you be there too? Will you go with us when He comes to take His own into His House of Gold? What a privilege it is to be on the journey there! You may come along too. You are welcome!

> *There is eternal, great compassion*
> *Surpassing ev'ry human thought;*
> *A tender-mercy, bringing sinners*
> *Into contact with the heart of God.*
> *From guilt it frees them,*
> *through His love,*
> *And guides them to God's House above.*
>
> *All sins of those who come believing*
> *In Jesus' blood, are washed away.*
> *God's message is: I am receiving*
> *The greatest sinner found today.*
> *God brings them -*
> *wondrous day of grace -*
> *To His eternal dwelling place.*